SUCCESSFUL PATIO CONTAINERS

**The *Gardening Which?*
guide to creating colourful
displays that last longer**

CONTENTS

INTRODUCTION

BUYING PLANTS   4

GETTING PLANTS OFF TO A GOOD START   6

A-Z OF PATIO PLANTS

INTRODUCTION

A patio is an extension of the house that is halfway between a room and a garden. If you are starting with a bare block of paving, think of arranging your patio very much as you might when furnishing a room. The chances are that you will want space for a table and chairs for *al fresco* dining, somewhere to put out a sun lounger and maybe even a barbecue. Having established the position of your basic furniture and the thoroughfares, you can then decide on containers and plants.

In this booklet we look at the best annuals and perennials for use in patio containers. For each we have indicated the position, compost, feeding and watering requirements using the following icons:

POSITION	**COMPOST**	**FEEDING**	**WATERING**
Full sun or sun for more than half the day	Equal parts multipurpose and sharp sand or grit	Once a month during the growing season	Will tolerate drying out for short periods
Light shade or some sun	Multipurpose compost	Once a fortnight in growing season	Water up to once a day in summer
Full shade	John Innes No2 compost	Once a week in growing season	Needs to be kept moist

BUYING PLANTS

Many of the plants in this booklet can be grown from seed. Some, such as alyssum, are very easy to grow without any special facilities. To grow a wide range of plants from seed you need a heated propagator with an adjustable thermostat for germination, a greenhouse for growing plants on, and a coldframe for hardening off plants ready for their life outdoors. Growing plants from seed is generally the most economical way if you want a lot of plants. However, where you want only a few specimens, or where the seed is expensive as in the case of F1 pelargoniums, buying seedlings or plantlets can be more cost-effective. At garden centres and shops, you'll find the best choice of seeds between January and April. Mail-order seed suppliers offer the latest varieties and a wider range. Their new catalogues come out around mid- to late October each year.

Many unusual tender perennials are now available as plantlets or 'tots'

Seedlings

Some tender perennials and bedding plants are sold as seedlings. These are sold in pots or small trays at garden centres in February and March and can also be ordered from the mail-order seed catalogues for early spring delivery. Seedlings overcome any problems that you might have with germinating the seed, but you still need to prick out the plants into trays or individual pots and grow them on somewhere warm and light.

Plantlets

These are sold under a variety of names including 'tots', 'plugs' and 'Jiffy sevens', but they are all seedlings or rooted cuttings, generally with two or three pairs of leaves. The peak season for plantlets at garden centres is February to early May when an enormous range of varieties is available, including many of the more unusual tender perennials. But they do work out more expensive than strips.

Bedding strips

Strips usually contain between six and twelve small plants which are ready to plant out. They become available from early April and are an ideal way of buying annual bedding plants. It's important to remember that these plants are tender and will need protection until the threat of frost has passed – late May or early June in most areas. If a late frost threatens, cover planted-up containers with horticultural fleece to protect them at night.

Individual pots

Large plants in individual pots will give a near instant effect, but are by far the most expensive option. However, large plants can provide a source of cuttings if you are looking to bulk up the stock quickly.

GETTING PLANTS OFF TO A GOOD START

Planting a tub

Crocks are not essential if you use good-quality compost, though they do add weight and stability. Cover large drainage holes to prevent the compost being washed out. If you are planting a large specimen, position the plant in its original pot on a layer of compost so that the surface is at the correct level. Fill the new container with compost while the pot is still in place, firming the compost down well around the edges. Finally, remove the pot and insert the plant into the ready-made hole in its new container. Leave at least 2.5cm (1in) clear at the rim to allow for watering. With annual displays, start in the middle and work outwards, cramming in as many plants as will fit. Water all plants thoroughly before and after planting. Soak plants in a bucket of water if they look dry before you plant them.

Hanging baskets

Wire baskets Traditional baskets made of plastic-coated wire have large holes, making planting through the sides straightforward. They can dry out very quickly but this can be overcome by lining them with polythene.

Self-watering baskets These are more like plastic bowls with a water reservoir built into the bottom. A piece of matting draws water up to the compost as it dries out.

Plastic baskets You can buy plastic replicas of wire baskets, but these often tend to have narrow gaps in the sides, which makes them difficult to plant in the same way.

Half-baskets and mangers

These contain only half the volume of a round basket, so they need more frequent watering.

Liners

Sphagnum moss is the traditional liner for baskets, but its collection can pose an ecological threat to peat bogs. Recycled wool and cotton are easy to plant and some have a polythene inner lining to aid moisture retention. Coconut fibre liners are similar, but made of a much coarser material. Foam liners are more difficult to slit when planting the sides and, like simple polythene liners, tend to look unsightly until the plants cover them. Preformed wood-fibre liners are more difficult to plant up at the sides, though they are useful where you want to have a succession of plantings as they can be lifted out and replaced with another pre-planted liner.

Which size basket?

The larger the basket, the easier it is to keep watered. Larger baskets also produce better displays. The drawback is that cost increases with size. The best compromise is a 35cm (14in) basket.

Place a circle of polythene in the base to retain moisture

To plant the sides, push the top growth out from inside

Leave the compost surface concave for easy watering

AGERATUM

POSITION   COMPOST   FEEDING   WATERING

Flowering from June to September, the dwarf varieties are best for containers because they tend to be the most uniform and free-flowering. The blue are the most striking and most popular. White ones can look unsightly if not regularly deadheaded as the flowers turn brown when they fade. Ageratums generally perform best in fine summers and tolerate becoming quite dry at the roots, but cannot withstand prolonged drought. They make an attractive edging for large mixed plantings and are good fillers.

Propagation Sow seed at 15°C (60°F) in March or early April, lightly covering the seed with compost.

Troubleshooting Flowers, particularly the white varieties, are prone to rotting in wet weather. Mildew can be a problem if watered infrequently.

Which variety? Dwarf, free-flowering varieties, growing 10-15cm (4-6in) in height: 'Adriatic' (mid-blue); 'Blue Champion' (mid-blue); 'Light Blue Champion' (paler); 'Blue Danube' (lavender blue); and 'Pacific' (violet-blue).

Ageratum 'Adriatic'

ALYSSUM

POSITION   COMPOST   FEEDING   WATERING

Modern varieties form neat mounds of densely branched stems, reaching 10-15cm (4-6in) in diameter. On well-grown plants, the leaves are almost hidden by the honey-scented flowers. They flower from June to September, prefer full sun and tolerate occasional drying out.

Propagation Sow from February to March at 10-13°C (50-55°F) and harden off before planting out from April onwards. Seeds can be sown outdoors in April.

Troubleshooting Stunted growth and white blisters on the undersides of leaves are a sign of downy mildew. Remove badly affected plants and spray with fungicide.

Which variety? 'Aphrodite' (bright mixture of seven colours including lilac, purple, cream, lemon and apricot); 'Creamery' (pale creamy-yellow); 'Easter Bonnet' (purple, rose, lavender and white); 'Morning Mist' (pastel mixture of pinks, purples, cream and white); 'Oriental Night' (rich purple flowers); 'Snow Crystals' (larger-than-average white flowers, compact).

Alyssum 'Creamery'

ARCTOTIS

POSITION   COMPOST   FEEDING   WATERING

From June to October, these exceptionally showy tender perennials produce large daisy flowers up to 10cm (4in) across. The flowers are borne singly on stout stems above a neat mound of divided foliage and are good for cutting.

Propagation Take stem cuttings from late spring to late summer. Seed can be sown under cover in early spring at a temperature of 18-21°C (65-70°F), though cuttings are necessary to propagate named varieties.

Troubleshooting Arctotis dislike overwatering and good drainage is essential. Aphids: spray with pirimicarb (Rapid).

Which variety? The many colourful forms now available are all forms of *Arctotis* x *hybrida*. 'African Sunrise' (bright orange flowers and grey-green foliage). 'Flame' (red-orange flowers and grey-green leaves). 'Midday Sun' (orange flowers which shade to yellow in the centre, and silvery-grey foliage). 'Tangerine' (pale-apricot-orange flowers and silver-grey leaves). 'Apricot' is similar. 'Wine' (unusual pinky-red flowers, and silver-grey leaves).

Arctotis 'Flame'

ARGYRANTHEMUM

POSITION COMPOST FEEDING WATERING

These tall, upright, bushy plants make ideal centrepieces in large containers, while single plants are also useful fillers. The daisy-like flowers come in a wide range of colours and are borne in profusion from late spring through summer and into autumn.

Propagation Semi-ripe cuttings taken in late summer are most successful, though cuttings can also be taken from the soft new shoots of overwintered plants in early spring.

Troubleshooting Pinch out the growing tips regularly to avoid the plant becoming thin and lanky.

Which variety? 'Blizzard', also called 'Mini-Snowflake', (compact grower bearing small, double, white flowers). 'Brontës' (single, primrose-yellow flowers, compact plant). 'Edelweiss' (compact plant with double, white flowers). 'Jamaica Primrose' (vigorous, single variety with butter-yellow flowers). 'Jamaica Snowstorm' (single white daisies with yellow centre, compact plant).'Vancouver' (deep dusky-pink flowers).

'Jamaica Primrose' and 'Vancouver'

11

BEGONIA

POSITION   COMPOST FEEDING WATERING

Begonia semperflorens is a dwarf species growing to 15-23cm (6-9in) high which is suited to edging containers and for window-boxes. It forms a neat, bushy plant of rounded, glossy leaves which are either fresh green or with purple or bronze tints. Flowers are borne on short stems from mid-summer to autumn. They thrive in sun or partial shade, but they will not tolerate drying out.

Propagation Sow seed in late winter at 18°C (65°C). Do not cover seed with compost as it needs light to germinate. You can take cuttings from plants throughout the summer.

Troubleshooting Avoid splashing water on the foliage, particularly when the plant is in full sun, as it can scorch.

Which variety? If you want to grow your own from seed, the following mixtures have all done well in *Gardening Which?* trials: 'Cocktail' (shades of pink plus white with reddish or bronze foliage); 'Party Fun' (pink, red and white with green or bronze foliage); 'Treasure Trove' (red, pink, and pink-and-white flowers, green or bronze foliage).

Begonias thrive in sun or partial shade

12

BELLIS

POSITION   COMPOST FEEDING WATERING

Bellis perennis is a perennial that forms low, neat rosettes of fresh green foliage. It produces colourful flowers on short stems from April to June. They are ideal for containers, window-boxes and hanging baskets and make splendid companions for hyacinths or dwarf tulips.

Propagation Sow seed thinly in a nursery bed outdoors in mid-summer. Pot the seedlings into 7.5cm (3in) pots when large enough to handle. Transplant to their flowering positions in early autumn, spaced 15cm (6in) apart.

Troubleshooting Generally trouble-free.

Which variety? Most varieties have double, pompon-type blooms. 'Carpet' is available as a mixture of red, rose-pink and white flowers, or sometimes as individual colours. 'Habenera Mixed' has red, pink and white flowers with needle-like petals; an unusual contrast to the pompon-type flowers. 'Pomponette' has small, tightly formed blooms in red, rose-pink and white. 'Radar series' has large pompon flowers available in mixed or single colours.

Spring display including bellis

13

BIDENS

A vigorous tender perennial which soon forms a spreading mass of trailing stems covered with golden-yellow, single daisy flowers and finely divided green leaves. This versatile plant can be grown in a hanging basket to form a cascade of stems, either on its own or combined with other plants, or as groundcover in a sunny, well-drained spot. Its thin stems can thread through the branches of the larger plant to spangle it with yellow flowers. Bidens thrives in a sun-baked spot. Like all plants, it is best not to let the compost dry out, but if this does happen you can rejuvenate plants quickly by soaking the rootball in a bucket of water.

Propagation Cuttings can be taken in spring or summer. Alternatively, the shoots can be pegged down and layered in pots of compost. Rooting takes only a few weeks. Plants can be raised from seed, though they take some time to flower well in their first season.

Troubleshooting Generally trouble-free.

Which variety? Two very similar species are available; they are *B. aurea* and *B. ferulifolia*.

Bidens and helichrysum

14

BRACHYSCOME

POSITION COMPOST FEEDING WATERING

A free-flowering plant producing many small daisy flowers amongst feathery foliage, *B. multifida* has a spreading, slightly bushy habit which makes it excellent for hanging baskets and for the edges of containers. *B. iberidifolia* (Swan river daisy) has slightly coarser leaves and a bushy habit up to 23cm (9in) high.

Propagation Sow seed of *B. iberidifolia* in early spring at 18°C (65°F). Cuttings of *B. multifida* root well in summer.

Troubleshooting Generally trouble-free.

Which variety? *B. iberidifolia* (Swan river daisy) is a half-hardy annual with an upright habit. Slightly scented flowers, up to 2.5cm (1in) across are borne from June to October. 'Purple Splendour' (deep bluish-purple); 'Blue Splendour' (mid-blue blooms); 'White Splendour' (pure white).

   B. multifida is a tender perennial with finely divided foliage and small flowers. The flowers of the species are mid-blue, 'Blue Mist' (pale blue); 'Lemon Mist' (pale yellow); 'Pink Mist'(pale lilac-pink).

Brachyscome 'Purple Splendour'

15

BRASSICAS

POSITION   COMPOST FEEDING WATERING

Ornamental brassicas with decorative foliage have rapidly become fashionable for autumn and winter displays. Leaf colours offer a wide range of variations in shade and leaf shapes. Although edible, they have a bitter taste, so are best used only as a colourful garnish.

Propagation Sow seed in late May or June at 15°C (60°F). Pot up seedlings individually and keep them well watered and fed. Plants prefer cool growing conditions.

Troubleshooting Slug damage can be a problem so it is worth taking precautions at an early stage.

Which variety? Cabbage 'Northern Lights' is an excellent F1 hybrid with rounded heads of leaves that are frilled at the edges and which come in a range of striking colours. Seed available either as a mixture or in separate colours. Kales have a more open habit and feathery leaves, a tendency which is most pronounced in varieties such as 'Red Feather' (red upper leaves, purple-red lower), and 'White Feather' (cream on top, green below).

Winter display of ornamental brassicas

CHRYSANTHEMUMS

POSITION   COMPOST   FEEDING   WATERING

Mini-chrysanthemums form tiny pompon flowers on top of 15cm (6in) high plants. They are ideal for providing instant colour in mid-summer up until the frosts. The orange and yellow ones create a similar effect to French marigolds, but you can also get a range of pastel and earthy shades. When you buy them, it is best to pot four or five plants into a 15cm (6in) pot and move them around the patio to wherever colour is lacking. Keep well-watered and liquid-feed regularly for the best display. It is worth deadheading chrysanths regularly, especially after a spell of wet weather, to keep the display looking fresh. This is particularly important with pale-coloured varieties. Plants are best discarded when they have flowered.

Propagation Plants are generally treated to keep them dwarf so this is not worthwhile.

Troubleshooting Generally trouble-free as temporary summer plants.

Which variety? Usually sold as 'mini-mums', 'garden mums' or bedding chrysanths in a range of attractive colours.

Mini-mums add instant colour

COLEUS

POSITION   COMPOST FEEDING WATERING

Coleus are grown for their colourful leaves which come in
myriad bright shades and patterns. Although perennials,
they tend to become leggy after more than one season so
it's best to take cuttings at least once a year. To get the
best display, keep the plants well watered and fed and
pinch out the growing tips every week or two. If left to
their own devices, they form rather insignificant woolly
clusters of flowers and then rapidly go downhill.

Propagation Growing from seed is one way to get a range
of different colours cheaply. Sow from February to April at
15°C (60°F). Shoot tips readily root in compost or water
throughout late spring and summer.

Troubleshooting Generally
trouble-free.

Which variety? Mixtures
such as 'Wizard Mixed'
will give you a wide range
of different colours. If you
have a particular planting
scheme in mind, try single
colours: 'Volcano' (bright
red); or 'Scarlet Poncho'
(red, gold edge). 'Sabre' is
a dwarf mixture growing
only 15cm (6in) tall.

Fine foliage colours of coleus

18

DIANTHUS

POSITION   COMPOST   FEEDING   WATERING

Indian pinks flower from mid-summer until the first frosts.
Though often referred to as annual pinks, they are
perennials, but tend to look rather tatty in their second year
unless propagated from cuttings. Deadhead regularly.
Flowering may be delayed if the weather remains dull.

Propagation Sow in March at 15°C (60°F) or take
cuttings in September. Overwinter in a cool greenhouse.

Troubleshooting Waterlogging can easily kill the plants.
Always use a well-drained compost and raise the container
off the ground so water can drain freely.

Which variety? All of these are 20cm (8in) tall unless
otherwise stated. 'Carpet series' (mixture or single
colours). 'Colour Magician'
(turns from white to deep
rose-pink, 25cm/10in).
'Magic Charms' (mixture
of red, pink and white).
'Raspberry Parfait'
(crimson, darker centre).
'Strawberry Parfait' (rose-
pink with a scarlet centre).
'Snowfire' (bright scarlet
petals with a broad white
margin). 'Telstar' (mixture
of white, reds and pinks).

Dianthus 'Raspberry Parfait'

EURYOPS

POSITION   COMPOST   FEEDING   WATERING

These upright, bushy plants grow to 45-60cm (18-24in) high and often taller if they are more than one year old. They develop a short section of clear stem at the base, which makes them perfect for planting in the centre of a large container. Bright yellow, daisy-like blooms are borne singly on slender stems throughout summer, though flowering tends to be limited in periods of dull weather.

Propagation Take cuttings in mid- to late summer.

Troubleshooting Established plants dislike root disturbance, so overwintered plants are best top-dressed with some fresh potting compost and controlled-release fertiliser (eg Osmocote) rather than being repotted.

Which variety? All species produce bright yellow flowers. *E. acraeus* has whorls of silvery leaves and forms a neat dome shape. *E. chrysanthemoides* has glossy, bright green leaves which are rather like those of an oak tree. *E. pectinatus* has finely divided, grey-green foliage. This species tends to flower best in the early part of the summer.

Euryops pectinatus

20

FELICIA

POSITION   COMPOST   FEEDING   WATERING

These neat, rounded, bushy plants produce many small, daisy-like flowers on slender stems above a mound of fresh green foliage. They flower from June to September and are ideal as a low centrepiece to a hanging basket, window-box or a small container. Most varieties bear flowers which are a beautiful shade of sky-blue with golden centres. Felicias are best overwintered in a frost-free place. Lightly prune overwintered plants in April.

Propagation Take cuttings from mid- to late summer.

Troubleshooting Generally trouble-free.

Which variety? *F. amelloides* is the species that is generally available, and there are also several hybrids. 'Astrid Thomas' and 'Santa Anita' both have larger blue flowers than the species. 'Read's Blue' has similar flowers, with leaves that are more rounded than those of the species. 'Read's White' has white flowers.

    F. amelloides 'Variegata' has leaves which are attractively green-and-white variegated; this contrasts well with its blue flowers.

Felicia amelloides 'Santa Anita'

21

FUCHSIA

POSITION   COMPOST   FEEDING   WATERING

Fuchsias come in an enormous range of colours and sizes.
Upright fuchsias are easiest to grow in bush form, where
they will attain a height and spread of up to 60cm (24in).
Trailing fuchsias are perfect for hanging baskets where
their large, showy blooms can cascade freely.

Fuchsias are best grown in light shade as direct sun will
scorch the leaves and bleach the flowers. The exceptions
are those with orange flowers and bronze leaves, which
revel in sunny positions. To ensure bushy, flower-laden
plants, pinch out the growing tips of young plants.
Fuchsias need to be kept moist and well fed. The best way
to feed them in hanging baskets and tubs is to add
controlled-release fertiliser (eg Osmocote) granules when
planting up and supplement
this with a weekly tomato
feed from August.
Deadhead regularly.

Propagation Take cuttings
in late summer for
overwintering, or from new
shoots in March to produce
plants that flower the same
year. 'Chimes' and
'Florabelle', can be grown
from seed. Sow in January
at 21-23°C (70-75°F).

Fuchsia 'Southgate' and chlorophytum

Troubleshooting

Aphids: spray with pirimicarb (Rapid). Whitefly: spray with permethrin bifenthrin every four days for several weeks or until no more adults appear. Grey mould: remove infected shoots and place the plant in a more open spot. Rust: spray Nimrod-T, and discard any badly infected plants.

Fuchsia 'Thalia'

Which variety?

Upright types 'Ballerina' (single – white in the centre with red sepals). 'Chimes' (range of colours from seed). 'Dollar Princess' (hardy, double – dark blue centres and swept-back, scarlet-red sepals). 'Pink Spangles' (semi-double – white centres and horizontal dark pink sepals). 'Thalia' (tender – tubular deep orange-red flowers, dark purplish-red foliage). 'Winston Churchill' (double – purple in the centre with red sepals).

Trailing types 'Cascade' (single – purple in the centre with soft pink sepals). 'Florabelle' (red sepals with purple petals). 'Harry Gray' (semi-double – white in the centre, with soft pink and white sepals). 'Golden Marinka' (single – deep red). 'La Campanella' (semi-double – lilac in the centre with white sepals). 'Marinka' (single – deep red). 'Patio Princess' (white flowers that are veined with pink and rose-pink sepals).

GAZANIA

POSITION   COMPOST   FEEDING   WATERING

From June to September, this showy tender perennial bears
large daisy flowers up to 7.5cm (3in) across on stout stems
above slender leaves. Gazanias thrive in a very sunny spot,
preferring well-drained soil. They have a neat habit of 23-
30cm (9-12in) high and a spread of up to 30cm (12in).

Propagation Take cuttings in July or August to propagate
the varieties named below. Seed can be sown in January or
February at 15°C (60°F).

Troubleshooting Generally trouble-free, though grey
mould may be a problem in long spells of wet weather.

Which variety? 'Aztec' (cream petals, with maroon
central band, and silver foliage). 'Bicton Orange' (golden
petals with a central orange
stripe, and silver foliage).
'Blackberry Ripple' (pink
petals with a purple central
stripe and silvery leaves).
'Blaze of Fire' (orange
flowers, petals turn gold at
tips, green foliage).
'Sunbeam' (deep orange,
darker in the centre, silver
foliage). 'Tiger' (rusty-
brown flowers, darker
centre, silvery foliage).

Gazanias make ideal single-subject pots

GLECHOMA

POSITION   COMPOST   FEEDING   WATERING

Although this trailing plant is a hardy perennial, it is widely
used in hanging baskets and window-boxes to complement
seasonal flowering plants. It forms long trails of slender
stems clothed with kidney-shaped, toothed leaves which are
attractively variegated with green and white. Small clusters
of lilac-blue flowers are often borne in the leaf axils in June
and July, though the ornamental foliage is this plant's main
attraction. The stems can grow up to 90cm (36in) long, so
it needs plenty of hanging space in order to be shown to its
best advantage. Keep well watered and feed every couple
of weeks throughout the growing season. It thrives equally
well in sun or partial shade.

Propagation Stems of the plant can easily be layered
throughout summer.
Cuttings can be taken in
spring and summer.

Troubleshooting It gets
very straggly if allowed to
dry out. Trim plants hard
back if this happens.

Which variety? Only one
species and variety is
generally available. It was
formerly known as *Nepeta
hederacea* 'Variegata'.

Glechoma thrives in sun or shade

HELICHRYSUM

POSITION   COMPOST   FEEDING   WATERING

This attractive foliage plant is widely used in summer plantings to complement flowering plants. With a spreading, freely branching habit, it is ideal for hanging baskets, window-boxes and the edges of containers. It may be necessary to trim the shoots to restrict its growth.

Overwinter plants by trimming back to leave at least 15cm (6in). In late February or March, give them a bit of extra warmth to encourage new growth to make cuttings.

Propagation Take cuttings from spring to late summer.

Troubleshooting Neglected plants can be rejuvenated by cutting hard back.

Which variety? *H. microphyllum* has tiny silver leaves and a neat, compact habit. *H. petiolare* has rounded, silver-grey leaves on a vigorous, spreading plant. 'Goring Silver' has small silvery leaves. 'Limelight' ('Aureum') has lime-yellow foliage. 'Roundabout' has small leaves which are variegated with grey and gold. 'Variegatum' has leaves which are variegated with gold and olive green.

Helichrysum petiolare

26

IMPATIENS

POSITION   COMPOST   FEEDING   WATERING

Busy lizzies thrive in full shade, which makes them
particularly useful for brightening up dull corners. They
also do well in sun, but it is preferable to avoid very hot
sites. They flower from June to October and a low-
growing, slightly spreading habit makes them excellent for
all containers, as well as in borders. New Guinea hybrids
are larger plants (23-38cm/9-15in) with attractive foliage.

Propagation Sow seed at 21-25°C (70-75°F) from January
to March on the surface of the compost as light is needed
for germination. Cover pots or trays with clinging film.

Troubleshooting Aphids can be a problem. Over-watering
causes older leaves to turn yellow and fall.

Which variety?
   Single flowers 'Accent',
'Deco', 'Expo', 'Swirl',
'Tempo', 'Mega Orange
Star', and 'Super Elfin'.
   Doubles 'Blackberry Ice',
'Ballerina', 'Dapper Dan',
'Madame Pompadour',
'Orange Sunrise', 'Peach
Ice', 'Raspberry Ripple' and
'Snowflake'.
   New Guinea 'Spectra',
'Tahiti', 'Tango'.

Busy lizzies flower well in shade

LANTANA

POSITION   COMPOST   FEEDING   WATERING

Most varieties have a rounded habit and are ideal in pots
on their own or as part of a larger planting in tubs. The
spreading types make attractive hanging basket plants.
Most have dark green leaves with toothed edges. They
flower from June to September and are all evergreens, so
they should be kept growing through the winter. Keep just
moist in good light at a minimum temperature of 7°C
(45°F). Prune hard back in spring. All parts are poisonous.

Propagation Take cuttings from mid- to late summer.

Troubleshooting Generally trouble-free.

Which variety? Most plants are hybrid forms of *Lantana
camara* and are generally sold by flower colour: yellow,
orange, red, pink and white.
'Aloha' (bright yellow, pale
green and cream-variegated
foliage). 'Cocktail' (yellow,
redden as they age). *L.
montevidensis* has a low,
spreading habit, growing
15cm (6in) tall and up to
90cm (36in) across. It
produces clusters of rosy-
lilac flowers throughout the
summer. White and yellow
forms are also available.

Lantana flowers all summer long

28

LOBELIA

POSITION   COMPOST   FEEDING   WATERING

Bushy lobelias form tight mounds up to 15cm (6in) high
and are covered with tiny flowers from June to September.
They make good edging plants in containers and raised
beds. Trailing types are ideal at the edges of baskets.

Propagation Sow from January to March at 18°C (65°F).
Don't cover the tiny seeds as they need light to germinate.
Cover with clinging film to prevent seed drying out.

Troubleshooting Damping-off disease can affect tiny
seedlings: sow thinly and water with copper fungicide.

Which variety?

  Bushy types 'Cambridge Blue' (sky blue), 'Crystal
Palace' (deep blue), 'Mrs Clibran' (deep blue, white eye),
'Riviera Blue Splash' (white
with a blue throat), 'Riviera
Lilac' (lilac-pink), and
'String of Pearls' (blue, red
and white).

  Trailing types 'Cascade'
(blue, red, lilac and white),
'Fountain' (light blue,
crimson, lilac, rose and
white), 'Regatta' (rose/white
eye, lilac and shades of
blue), 'Sapphire' (deep blue,
white eye).

Lobelia 'Riviera Lilac'

29

LOTUS

POSITION   COMPOST   FEEDING   WATERING

These attractive plants form a cascading curtain of slender stems which can grow up to 90cm (36in) long. In cooler areas it is best to think of this as a foliage plant, as it only flowers freely (between June and September) during a long, hot summer. Lotus need good drainage but are reasonably drought-tolerant and do not require a lot of fertiliser. The dark red or orange blooms are produced in claw-like clusters. Overwinter plants without cutting them back, keeping them barely moist during winter.

Propagation Take cuttings from early to mid-summer.

Troubleshooting Trim back tatty-looking foliage.

Which variety? Three species of lotus are commonly available, though the similarity of their names can lead to some confusion. *L. berthelotii* produces long stems clad with fine, needle-like, silver leaves and bears dark red flowers. *L. berthelotii* x *maculatus* has pale green leaves and flowers a mixture of red and yellow. *L. maculatus* has pale green leaves and orange/yellow flowers.

Lotus maculatus

LYSIMACHIA

POSITION   COMPOST FEEDING WATERING

These trailing plants with handsome foliage are ideal for
hanging baskets, window-boxes and container edges.
Golden-yellow flowers are borne from June to September.
Lysimachia nummularia 'Aurea' (golden creeping Jenny)
is actually a hardy perennial, though it is widely used in
summer displays. It will grow in full sun providing you
keep the containers well-watered, though the leaves may
become bleached. *L. congestiflora* prefers a sunny position.

Propagation Layer *L. nummularia* 'Aurea' by pegging
down shoots into pots of compost. Take cuttings of
L. congestiflora in mid- to late summer.

Troubleshooting Generally trouble-free.

Which variety?

L. congestiflora ('Lissy')
forms a neat, pendulous
plant clothed with heart-
shaped leaves and yellow
flowers. *L. congestiflora*
'Outback Sunset' is similar,
but with gold and green
variegated foliage.
L. nummularia 'Aurea'
develops trailing stems with
small, rounded, pale yellow
leaves and yellow flowers.

Lysimachia flowers all summer

31

MARIGOLDS

POSITION

COMPOST

FEEDING

WATERING

The flower heads of these popular bedding plants are vividly coloured, mostly in shades of yellow and orange. They are borne from June to October on neat, upright plants above divided green leaves. African marigolds have the largest heads, up to 10cm (4in) across. Those of French marigolds are smaller but are often borne in greater numbers. Tagetes are similar to French marigolds though they grow slightly taller, and their looser habit makes them better suited to less formal groupings. Marigolds are ideal in containers and window-boxes.

Propagation African marigolds take 12 weeks or more to flower, so are best sown in February. French marigolds flower in 6 to 8 weeks and can be sown in April or early May. Sow tagetes from March to April. Germinate at 15-18°C (60-65°F).

Troubleshooting Grey mould can be a problem in prolonged spells of wet weather. Remove and destroy infected parts of the plant and spray with Bio Supercarb Systemic Fungicide to prevent the disease spreading.

'Inca Mixed'

Which variety?
African marigolds
(includes Afro-French hybrids): 'Discovery', grows 25cm (10in) high, blooms 8cm (3in) across, bright orange or yellow. 'Excel', grows 25-35cm (10-14in) high, blooms orange, golden-orange, lemon-yellow and primrose-yellow. 'Inca', grows 30cm (12in) high, blooms 10cm (4in) across, gold, orange and bright yellow. 'Vanilla', grows 30-35cm (12-14in) high, blooms creamy-yellow.

'Tangerine Gem'

French marigolds 'Alamo', grows 20-25cm (8-10in) high, double flowers – 'Alamo Flame' (orange/red), 'Alamo Harmony' (maroon/orange crest), 'Alamo Orange' (bright orange) and 'Alamo Yellow' (deep yellow). 'Boy', grows 16-20cm (6-8in) high, double flowers – 'Golden Boy' (golden-yellow), 'Harmony Boy' (gold with red crest), 'Orange Boy' (deep orange) and 'Yellow Boy' (lemon-yellow). 'Boy O'Boy' is a mixture of these varieties. 'Disco', grows 20-25cm (8-10in) high, single flowers – 'Disco Flame' (red/orange bicolour), 'Disco Orange' (warm orange), 'Disco Red' (dark red edged with gold) and 'Disco Yellow' (lemon-yellow).

Tagetes signata, plants grow up to 30cm (12in) high – 'Golden Gem' (gold), 'Lemon Gem' (lemon-yellow), 'Tangerine Gem' (orange).

NEMESIA

POSITION   COMPOST   FEEDING   WATERING

The annual varieties have an upright habit which makes
them ideal for tubs and window-boxes, while the tender
perennial forms have a more lax, spreading habit suited to
hanging baskets, as well as edging for larger containers.
Annuals may stop flowering after around eight weeks, but
will produce a second display if cut back after the first
flush. Perennials will flower continuously if deadheaded.

Propagation Sow annuals at 15-18°C (60-65°F) in March
or April. Take cuttings of perennials in spring or summer.

Troubleshooting Generally trouble-free.

Which variety?

Annuals 'Carnival Mixed' (red, blue and yellow).
'Galaxy Mixed' (blues and
pinks). 'KLM' (bicoloured;
rich blue and cream).
'Orange Prince' (vivid
orange). 'Red Ensign'
(bicoloured; white and red).

Perennials *N. caerulea*
(lilac-mauve, yellow
centre). 'Elliott's Variety'
(light blue, yellow eye).
N. denticulata 'Confetti'
(pictured). 'Innocence'
(white, with a yellow eye).

Nemesia 'Confetti'

NICOTIANA

POSITION   COMPOST   FEEDING   WATERING

Recent varieties have a neat, bushy habit with many blooms borne from June to September on short, stout stems that do not need any form of support. Most of these compact varieties tend not to be scented. Nicotianas are generally tough plants that will tolerate occasional drying out and do well in sun or light shade. Plants may survive the winter outdoors to flower a second year.

Propagation Sow at 18°C (65°F) from mid-February to March. Do not cover seed as it needs light to germinate.

Troubleshooting Aphids: spray with pirimicarb (Rapid).

Which variety? 'Domino' available as mixed or individual colours (white, lime-green, salmon-pink, red, pink with a white eye). 'Domino Picotee' (white, edged with rose-pink). Not scented. 25-30cm (10-12in). 'Havana Appleblossom' (rose-pink with white centre, darker edges). Weather resistant. Slightly scented. 38cm (15in). 'Havana Lime Green' similar to above (lime-green) 'Starship' (red, pink, burgundy and lime-green). Height 30cm (12in).

Nicotiana 'Domino Mixed'

NIGELLA

POSITION COMPOST FEEDING WATERING

An easy-to-grow annual with feathery foliage, saucer-shaped flowers and attractive seed heads, *Nigella damascena* is useful for sowing in a tub around a permanent shrub to provide summer colour or in a pot on its own. The flowers, which are borne between June and August, mostly come in blue or white, though pink and mauve shades are also available. They like a sunny position and should be kept moist to prolong flowering.

Propagation Sow seed direct in containers in March or April, covering lightly with compost. Alternatively, for larger and earlier-flowering plants, sow in pots or trays in a coldframe or cool greenhouse in September.

Troubleshooting Generally trouble-free.

Which variety? 'Miss Jekyll Blue' has large, semi-double, bright-blue flowers. 'Persian Jewels' has a mixture of semi-double pink, mauve, purple, blue and white flowers. 'Persian Rose' has rose-pink flowers. *N. hispanica* has slightly scented blue flowers with red stamens.

Nigella flowers longer if kept moist

OSTEOSPERMUM

POSITION   COMPOST   FEEDING   WATERING

Osteospermums produce large, daisy-like flowers about 5-7.5cm (2-3in) across which are borne individually on short stems. A few have variegated foliage, and others have distinctive petals which are spoon-shaped. Upright types are 45cm (18in) tall and spreading ones 20x45cm (8x18in). Both flower from June to September.

Propagation Take cuttings in growing season. Late summer is the best time to take cuttings for overwintering.

Troubleshooting Generally trouble-free.

Which variety?

Upright types 'Buttermilk' (creamy-yellow, dark centres). 'James Elliman' (deep purple). 'Pink Whirls' (deep pink, unusual spoon-shaped petals). 'Whirligig' (white, spoon-shaped petals, dark centre). 'Zulu' (deep yellow).

Spreading *O. ecklonis* 'Prostratum' (white, bluish-purple underneath). Hardier than most. 'Bodegas Pink' (pink, dark centre) cream-edged leaves. 'Gweek Variegated' (purple) cream and green foliage. 'Port Wine' (deep maroon).

Osteospermum 'Whirligig'

PANSY

POSITION   COMPOST   FEEDING   WATERING

Pansies are superb for providing colour in containers almost year-round. Winter-flowering varieties will bloom on and off during mild spells throughout the coldest months of the year, but they can be grown to flower during any period. The other types are best suited for spring and summer flowering. To ensure a good display of flowers, keep containers well watered at all times but never let the compost get waterlogged. Regular deadheading will increase the quantity and period of flowering. They do not like intense heat and do best in light shade during the hottest months of summer.

Propagation Sow seed at 15°C (60°F) in February to March for summer flowers, in May for winter blooms, or in September for a spring display. You can also propagate from cuttings, or by earthing up around the plants so that the individual stems take root.

Troubleshooting Fungal diseases can attack pansies and kill the whole plant, particularly in wet conditions. Always use fresh compost for pansies.

Winter pansy, hellebore, iris and bergenia

Which variety?

Varieties for spring and autumn flowers 'Chalon Giants Mixed' have ruffled blooms that give the effect of double flowers. They come in shades of lilac, violet, mahogany and yellow, with blotched centres. 'Imperial' series bears medium to large flowers in a range of attractive shades: 'Imperial Antique Shades' range from apricot through to rose, 'Imperial Frosty Rose' is rosy-purple and white, while 'Imperial Lavender Shades' range

Spring-flowering 'Padparadja'

from palest lavender to deep purple. 'Jolly Joker' has flowers which are a startling combination of orange and purple. 'Padparadja' is an unusual colour, with blooms that are uniform, bright, glowing orange.

Varieties for winter flowers 'Ultima' series offers a good colour selection including unusual shades, such as 'Ultima Chiffon', an attractive creamy-white with a bold rose blotch, and 'Ultima Sherbet' which is similar but has its white area tinged with rose-pink. 'Universal' series come in a huge range of colours including reds, blues, yellows and whites. Some have flowers with plain 'faces', others have a dark central blotch, and yet more have a coloured central blotch.

PELARGONIUM

POSITION COMPOST FEEDING WATERING

Pelargoniums, or geraniums as they are popularly known, are one of the most widely grown plants for containers and baskets. Their brightly coloured flowers, neat, compact habit and resistance to drought make them ideal for containers. Most of the varieties sold nowadays are F1 hybrids and are free-flowering. They love sunshine and will survive if you forget to water them occasionally. However, they do like regular feeding.

Plants can be overwintered in a frost-free place. If they are potted up individually and kept on a warm window-sill, flowers will often be produced right through the winter.

Propagation Take cuttings in early spring to provide plants for the current season, or in mid- to late summer to produce young plants for overwintering.

Seed can be sown from January to early April. Germinate at 21°C (70°F).

Troubleshooting Upright varieties are generally trouble-free. Ivy-leaved types are susceptible to oedema, which shows as

Summer collection of mixed pelargoniums

40

corky growths or blisters on the leaves.

Which variety?

Upright types The following are all F1 hybrids, and can be grown from seed or bought as plants in garden centres. 'Century' (pink, red, scarlet, violet-rose and white), zoned foliage. 'Maverick Star' (blush-pink, deeper pink at the edges – rose-pink eye). 'Multibloom' series (rose-pink, lavender-pink, red, salmon-pink, bright scarlet, scarlet with a white eye, and white). 'Orange Appeal' (bright orange). 'Raspberry Ripple' (salmon-pink, heavily flecked with red). 'Video' series (red, salmon, pink, and white with a pink blush).

Pelargonium, senecio and osteospermum

Trailing types 'Breakaway' (red and salmon-pink). 'Summer Showers' (red, pink, lavender, magenta and white). *P. peltatum* recommended varieties include: 'Beauty of Eastbourne' (cerise-red); 'Crocodile', attractive yellow patterned foliage; 'L'Elegante' (single, white) cream-edged leaves; 'Mini Cascade Red' (single, red); 'Rouletta' (semi-double, white edged with cerise) 'Snow Queen' (double white, red centres).

Continental trailing types 'Balcon' (also called 'Decora' or 'Cascade'). Flower clusters are fairly small but are borne in great profusion on loosely trailing stems (lilac, pink, red and white).

PETUNIA

POSITION

COMPOST

FEEDING

WATERING

Petunias are popular bedding plants which flower with large, exuberant, brightly coloured blooms from June to September. With a compact, bushy habit and above average drought-tolerance, these petunias are excellent for use in containers. Trailing petunias are perfect for baskets.

Propagation Take cuttings of perennials from spring to late summer. Sow seed in March at 15-18°C (60-65°F).

Troubleshooting Control aphids, as they spread viruses.

Which variety?

Bushy types 'Aladdin' hybrids (nine colours). 'Dream' hybrids (six colours). 'Duo Dolly Mixed' (double, five colours). 'Joy' hybrids (seven colours). 'Mirage Reflections' (five shades of pink).

Trailing types 'Million Bells' (blue and pink, golden eye), 'Purple Wave' (purple). 'Supercascade Improved Mixed' (ten colours).

Surfinias (colours as named): 'Blue Vein', 'Hot Pink', 'Pink Mini', 'Pink Vein', 'Purple', 'Purple Mini', 'Violet Blue' and 'White'.

'Mirage Reflections'

PLECTRANTHUS

POSITION   COMPOST   FEEDING   WATERING

A vigorous trailing plant that is useful for providing foliage interest in hanging baskets and tall containers. It produces stems that can grow up to 1.8m (6ft) in length, though it is generally best to pinch out the growing tips to encourage slightly shorter and more branching growths. The rounded leaves are attractively variegated with green and white, and they can be used as an excellent foil for many plants that have brightly coloured flowers.

Buying young plantlets in early spring is an economical way to purchase this thriving plant as you can then increase your stock from cuttings. Overwinter at 7°C (45°F) as plants or rooted cuttings.

Propagation Cuttings can be taken from spring to late summer. Pinched-out shoot tips will root within a week or two.

Troubleshooting Generally trouble-free.

Which variety?
P. forsteri 'Marginatus' is the variety sold as a patio plant. Other forms of plectranthus, such as *P. australis* (Swedish ivy), are sold as houseplants.

Plectranthus is a vigorous trailing plant

POLYANTHUS

POSITION   COMPOST   FEEDING   WATERING

They flower from January to May and are ideal for all sorts of containers. Pot-raised polyanthus can be added to tubs containing permanent plants to provide seasonal colour. Bright mixtures tend to look best with evergreens or on their own. Single colours make suitable companions for spring bulbs. Keep moist.

Propagation Sow in May or June at 15-18°C (60-65°F). Seed should be sown on the surface as it needs light to germinate. Cover pots or trays with clinging film.

Troubleshooting Birds, slugs and snails can be a problem. Plants that do not flower are usually a result of sowing too late or at too high a temperature.

Which variety? The following are all outdoor types: 'Crescendo' is the best of the hardy types, available as bright mixtures or single colours; 'Husky' bears large flowers in a mixture of colours on tough plants; 'Rainbow' is a short-stemmed variety in mixed colours, orange and red and lemon and gold, as well as single colours.

Polyanthus with euonymus and heather

44

SENECIO

POSITION   COMPOST   FEEDING   WATERING

These silvery-grey foliage plants are the perfect
companions for almost any flowers, toning down bright
colours and adding style to pastels. You can use them in
tubs, window-boxes or hanging baskets, where they are
ideal for edging or fillers. They are remarkably drought-
tolerant and require little feeding.

Light shade is no problem for the plants, but for the best
foliage colour, you need to grow them in sun. The plants
are perennials and will survive outdoors in sheltered
gardens through a mild winter. However, they tend to
become tall and straggly in their second year if not
regularly trimmed back. Yellow flowers are also produced
in the second year.

Propagation Sow from
February to April at 15°C
(60°F). You can also take
cuttings in spring.

Troubleshooting Generally
trouble-free.

Which variety? 'Cirrus'
has rounded greyish-silver
leaves. Height 30cm (12in).
'Silver Dust' has finely cut,
lace-like leaves in a bright
silver. Height 15cm (6in).

Senecio 'Silver Dust' and ageratum

VERBENA

POSITION

COMPOST

FEEDING

WATERING

The bush and trailing forms flower from June to September; both are excellent for containers. The trailing types are particularly suited to hanging baskets and container edges, where they combine well with other plants. Virtually all trailing types are tender perennials that are best bought as plants and propagated by cuttings, whereas bush types are annuals that can be raised from seed.

Propagation Sow bush types from January to March. All types can be propagated from cuttings in spring and summer.

Troubleshooting Mildew: spray with Nimrod-T before the disease spreads. Discard severely affected plants.

Which variety?

Trailing 'Aphrodite' (deep purple); 'Blue Cascade' (blue); 'Foxhunter' (red); 'Pink Parfait' (light and dark pink); 'Sissinghurst' (cherry-red).

Bush 'Amour' (pale pink, rose-pink, purple, and scarlet with a white eye); 'Blue Lagoon' (deep blue); 'Peaches and Cream' (coral, yellow, orange and salmon).

Verbena 'Peaches and Cream'

ZINNIA

POSITION   COMPOST   FEEDING   WATERING

From July to September zinnias produce bright, dahlia-like blooms on short, stocky plants. The flower size ranges from tiny single blooms to doubles over 10cm (4in) across. They thrive in hot, sunny conditions and are likely to be a disappointment in a cool, damp summer. They like a compost with plenty of nutrients, but will not suffer if you forget to water them occasionally. However, regular neglect will make them more vulnerable to mildew.

Propagation Sow seed at 21°C (70°F) in March or April. Grow on at minimum of 13°C (55°F).

Troubleshooting Seedlings are prone to damping off. Sow thinly and water with a copper fungicide. Mildew: spray with a fungicide at first signs of attack.

Which variety?

'Dreamland' (20cm/8in high) double flowers in red, yellow, pink, coral and ivory. 'Envy' (60cm/24in high) double lime-green blooms. 'Peter Pan' similar to 'Dreamland' but more colours. 'Star' (30cm/12in high) single blooms are more disease-resistant.

Zinnia 'Peter Pan'

HOW TO BECOME A MEMBER OF

Gardening
WHICH?

Gardening Which? is the ultimate gardening service.
Membership brings you:

- *Gardening Which?* magazine delivered to your door ten times a year
- FREE gardening advice by fax, e-mail or letter
- *Gardening Which?* OnHand – 24 hour advice on the telephone charged at the local rate
- Free seeds to try in your own garden
- FREE entry on weekdays to our gardens
- Discounts on our range of gardening books
- The chance to take part in our gardening trials

Gardening Which? is only available direct.
To try if FREE for three months, write to *Gardening Which?*
Dept C3896, Freepost, Hertford X, SG14 1YB or
FREEPHONE 0800 252 100 quoting C3896

Published by Which? Ltd
2 Marylebone Road, London NW1 4DF

First edition 1997
Reprinted July 1997, December 1997, April 1998

Copyright © 1997 Which? Ltd

This booklet contains extracts from *The Gardening Which? Guide to Patio and Container Plants*, available from Which? (freephone 0800 252 100) at £17.99, p&P free

ISBN 0 85202 681 1

Cover design by Creation Communications

Compiled and edited by
Jonathan Edwards, Martyn Hocking, Kate Hawkins and Hetty Don

Printed by Bath Colour Press
Reprinted by GSM Ltd, Swindon 1997
Reprinted by Business ColorPrint Ltd